# FRENCH BEADED FLOWERS I:
## A Guide for Beginners

Featuring Miniature and Small Arrangements

By Helen McCall

Illustrations by Pandora Frazier
Photography by Vic Cotto
Beadwork by Helen McCall
Layout by Christian A. Kennedy & Therese Spears
Editing by Therese Spears
Printed in the United States of America
ISBN 0-932255-04-3

For Information address:
        Promenade Publishing
        P.O. Box 2092
        Boulder, CO  80306
        A Division of Promenade Enterprises, Inc.

ACKNOWLEDGMENTS:

Special thanks go to my husband George McCall for all his support and encouragement, my daughter Mary McCall for her enthusiasm, David Bruton who went over my first draft with a very fine - tooth comb, Lydia Moore for her knowledge and friendship, and especially my mother-in-law, Katherine McCall, my first and best customer.

DEDICATION:

This book is dedicated to the memory of Catherine Stein.

# CONTENTS

# INTRODUCTION

The art of making beaded flowers has its origins in France during Victorian times when beads were used extensively on clothing and accessories. The peasants who beaded the clothing would set aside the odd size, color or shape of bead before sewing them on the garments. They would then take these beads and make flowers which were placed on church altars and on the graves of loved ones. The word "bead" comes from the Anglo-Saxon word "*bede*" which means prayer. Flower beading caught on and new designs for flowers could be found in many of the ladies' magazines. Then, as fashions changed and the demand for beaded clothing dropped, the art of flower beading faded away.

This book is written with the beginner in mind and contains only small or miniature arrangements. The first five flowers are what I call "learning" flowers. Each one focuses on a particular technique and will give the student a considerable amount of practice. As a reward for all that practice, you will have a beautiful little arrangement.

Since I can't be with you to guide your fingers and offer support, I hope that you will be your own gentle teacher and master the four main techniques before going on with the rest of the book. It is also important that you familiarize yourself with all the materials needed and that you read and understand the techniques and directions before beginning. Each of the flowers chosen for this book has something unique to offer which will help when you start designing your own.

Not all these flowers are my own designs. The thistle, iris, and the African violet, were designed by my late teacher, Catherine Stein, as was the poppy, which I slightly changed. My friend Lydia Moore, provided help and the designs for the Baby's Tears, Baby's Breath and Calla Lily.

# MATERIALS

## BEADS:

Beaded flowers are made exclusively with glass seed beads. These beads come primarily from Czechoslovakia, Japan and France and are available either loose or strung on hanks. Hanks are usually a group of 10 to 12 strands of beads which are 18 to 20 inches long and should be used almost exclusively because is much quicker to transfer the beads from the thread to the wire. Seed beads come in a variety of sizes ranging from 9°, the largest, to 18°, the smallest. 11° is the size used for most flowers. Since it is the most popular size, the selection of colors is greatest.

Many of the flowers in this book use the smaller 14° bead. These beads may be difficult to find, particularly in the color you want. If you cannot find 14° beads, it is possible to substitute the larger 11° bead. Wherever a flower calls for 14° beads in this book, I have noted a substitute for 11°. There may be some difference in the final appearance of the flower, but it will be just as beautiful!

The following is a brief description of the variety of seed beads available.

Ceylon: Opaque with a pearly finish. Less formal.
Charlotte: Occasional facets in an solid opaque.
French beads: Semi-opaque, smoky looking, opalescent.
Greasy: Semi-transparent with a semi-gloss.
Iridescent: A rainbow-like effect - - as in soap bubbles.
Iris: Can be transparent or opaque with a rainbow-like play of colors. Metallic looking with a rainbow - like play of colors.
Lined: Clear or transparent on outside, color on inside. Occasionally purple may fade. More formal.
Luster: Bright, shiny, semi-transparent, with a high gloss.
Opalescent: A milky iridescence - like an opal.
Opaque: Often called chalk - - solid in color, considered informal.
Silver Lined Rocaille: A mirrored effect coming from the center of the bead.
Transparent: Clear or colored bead that light can pass through. Will not fade. Formal.
2X: 2 cuts around the sides.
3X: 3 cuts around the sides creating a sparkle effect. Very beautiful on a formal flower.
White heart: White on inside - - different color on outside. Informal.
Pony: Similar to the seed bead only larger (4mm).

## WIRE:

There are several different types of wire used in the making of beaded flowers, and are usually available in craft stores. The wire, except for stem wire comes on spools with the sizes marked by gauge: the larger the number, the thinner the wire.

Goldine: A soft brass wire. The sizes used most often in this book are #26, #28, and #32.

Enameled: This is a coated wire and comes in a variety of colors. Green wire in size #28 and #26 is used in this book. It is a very sturdy wire and is good for making big leaves.

Ligature: Some beaders prefer to use a #007 ligature wire instead of the #32 or #34 goldine, for lacing and binding since it is very thin and very strong. This wire can be ordered from a cooperative orthodontist.

Stem Wire: This is a straight wire used for mounting flowers. The sizes used are #14, #16 and #18 depending on the heaviness of the flower.

**FLORAL TAPE:**

Floral tape comes in a variety of colors on 1/2" wide rolls and becomes tacky when stretched. The colors used in flower beading are light green for most flower stems, dark green on beaded trees and brown on terminal branches.

**CLAY:**

The best material to use for "planting" arrangements is floral clay, plasteline or modeling clay which will not harden. Styrofoam will not hold up flowers for very long.

**MOSS:**

This is sometimes called sheet moss and is used to cover the clay on top of the container. It can be purchased in several different varieties at a craft store. I also enjoy getting my own moss from the yard and from rocks at a nearby creek. If you do gather your own moss, let it dry in a dark place for several days and the nice dark green color will stay for a long time. Little stone chips from the pet store are a good alternative for covering the clay.

**CRAFT GLUE:**

A small amount of craft glue such as Elmer's or 527, is used on top of the floral clay to help hold the moss in place.

**CONTAINERS:**

Let your imagination and the size of the arrangement determine the type of container you use. Some people like to use porcelain or brass for their flowers, while others like little baskets, pottery bowls or miniature clay pots. Clear glass can be used, but it should be lined with moss anchored to the bottom with clay before packing the container. Be very careful when packing the clay in to a glass or porcelain container to avoid breakage. I have found that for miniature arrangements saki cups, lotus bowls, votive candle holders and tiny clay pots are the perfect size and not too expensive.

**EQUIPMENT:**

Wire cutters: Small diagonals will do.
Pliers: a) Small needle nose with ridges for better gripping; and (b) Heavy duty for cutting thick wire.
Awl: Called a scratch awl in hardware stores — a 3"one will do. This is used to help straighten crimped wire and to make holds in floral clay.
6" ruler: For use in measuring beads and wire.
Scissors: A small pair is needed for cutting thread and floral tape.
Container: A necessity for holding your supplies. A shoe box with a lid is perfect for starting out. The lid is used to hold your work over and will catch any spills. Yes, there will be split beads! It is also helpful to draw the various measurements in the lid as an easy guide.
Spool Holder: A block of wood approximately 4-1/2" wide by 9" long into which three 5" threaded bolts are drilled 2-1/2" apart. Wooden dowels may be used instead of the threaded bolts. They can be glued into holes drilled in the block of wood. This spool holder is not necessary, but it sure is helpful.

# INSTRUCTIONS AND TECHNIQUES

The following information covers everything from stringing beads onto the wire to planting your finished arrangement. The techniques listed below start with ones that are easier to master and end with those that are more difficult. Correspondingly, the first five flowers described are what I call learning flowers and will help the beginner to master each technique before going on.

Before beginning the first learning flower, please read the directions on beading and knotting the wire, the technique for that particular flower and the instructions. Have all your beads, wires and tools ready. At times your fingers may feel like thumbs, but that will pass with each bead you wire and each leaf or petal you make. Another problem beginning beaders experience, especially the overly enthusiastic ones, is that all those "thumbs" are going to hurt. That can be fixed by wrapping them with adhesive tape. The only real cure, though, is to continue beading and eventually those fingers will toughen up.

## GENERAL INSTRUCTIONS

### Beading the wire

Most wire comes on either plastic or metal spools and has little holes in the top for securing the wire. It is a good idea, however, to wrap a twist tie through the central hole and around the outside of the spool. This will prevent the wire, especially on a new spool, from spiraling off. Cut the wire on the diagonal to make a sharp point. Always keep the wire straight. Never cut the wire from the spool until you are finished with the leaf or petal, or if you need to add more beads.

(1)

Before beading the wire, it is helpful to put a piece of tape around the top strands of the hank of beads. Although they are tied together, the threads can pull out very easily and beads will be lost. After taping the hank, pull one end of a strand of beads from the hank and wrap the thread around the forefinger of your left hand, or right if you're left handed (fig. 1).

The beads are in front of the finger and the thread wraps over the top and around the finger several times. The thread is then held between the thumb and middle finger. Pull the beads over your thumb and secure them in the palm of your hand with the last two fingers. The middle finger may be needed in the beginning to help hold the thread that is wrapped around your forefinger if the thread is too short (fig. 2).

(2)

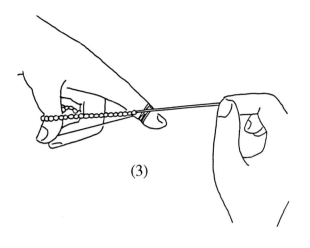

(3)

Gently insert the pointed wire into the beads (fig. 3). When you have an inch or so of beads on the wire, pull the thread out and let the beads slide down the wire. This procedure will get easier with practice, and it really is not as complicated as it sounds. If a bead doesn't fit, remove it from the strand. If your wire bends, straighten it so you can easily add more beads.

In order to keep the end of the thread from pulling out of the hank and losing beads, make a large knot near the end of the thread when half the beads have been transferred to the wire. Find the other end of the strand of beads, pull it from the hank and finish transferring the remaining beads onto the wire.

**Knotting the wire**

When enough beads have been transferred to the wire, "knot" the wire to prevent the beads from falling off. To do this, hold the wire in your right hand, with the end pointing towards the left. With the thumb and forefinger of your left hand, make a loop near the end of the wire (fig. 4).

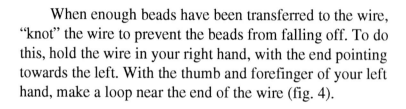

(4)

Insert your right forefinger in the "V" formed by the wires at the bottom of the loop. Hold the wires with your thumb on one side and your middle finger on the other side (fig. 5), and twist the loop towards you two times. Push the end of the wire back towards the loop so it won't stab you while you're working on the beads (fig. 6).

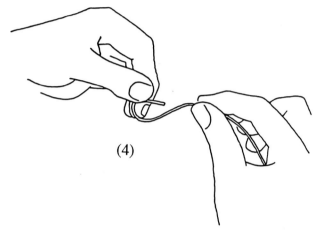

(5)

Do not cut the beaded wire from the spool. Almost all work is done with the beaded wire attached to the spool. If you run out of beads before the leaf or petal is finished, estimate how much wire you will need to complete your project, add about 4", and cut that amount from the spool. Add the required amount of beads to the end of the wire.

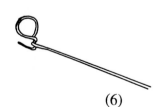

(6)

**Remember:**

Tape your hank of beads.
Cut the wire on the diagonal.
Keep your wire straight.
Make a big knot when you're halfway through the strand and pull the other end from the hank.
Knot your wire.
Do not cut the beaded wire from the spool.

## THE FOUR TECHNIQUES

The loop, four-row crossover, wraparound loop, and basic are the four main techniques used in making all petals and leaves. There is a flower dedicated to each technique in Chapter 3 which will give the beginner a lot of practice.

### Loop

Knot the end of your beaded wire and leave 3" of bare wire before starting the loop. Slide the amount of beads called for in the procedures to within 3" of the knot and form a loop. The procedure is the same as forming a loop for the knot. If just one loop is called for, twist the loop (fig. 7) two times towards you.

(7)

You can twist the other way and it will not make any difference — just be consistent. When the procedure states, "1" loop — 8 on 1 wire," measure 1" of beads, slide the rest of the beads back down the wire, make a loop and twist two times. Measure another 1" of beads and slide them to the base of the first loop. Make a loop. Hold this loop with your left thumb and finger and wrap the base of the loop one time with the feed wire (bare wire). Be sure the beads on your loop are tight. Continue in this manner until all the loops are made. Leave about 3" of bare wire after your last loop and cut from the spool. You may work your loops either to the right or to the left, whichever is more comfortable for you. Again, be consistent. It helps to bend the loops toward the knotted end of the wire when making more than 4 or 5. When making numerous loops, leave a little space between the loops, about, 1/16", every 3rd loop. This helps to keep the loops from curling too much.

The thistle and marigold are made entirely of loops. If you make one of these arrangements, you will definitely have the loop mastered!

## Four-row Crossover

Knot the end of your beaded wire and leave 3" of bare wire before starting. Measure the amount of beads called for in the procedures and make a loop. Twist the base of the loop twice, making sure the beads are tight. Squeeze the loop closed. Bring the beaded wire up in front of the closed loop. When the beads have reached the top of the loop, press them between the two rows. Place the bare wire over the top of the loop between two beads and press tightly to the back of the loop. Turn the petal over and fill the back of the loop with beads bringing the beaded wire back down to the base of the petal (fig. 8).

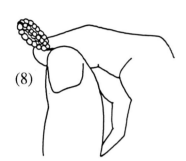

(8)

Twist the base of the loop twice. If making more than 1 four-row crossover on 1 wire, slide the required amount of beads to the first crossover and form a loop. Wrap the feed wire around the base of the loop 1 time and continue as above to form the four-row crossover. Wrap the feed wire again around the base 1 time. When finished with the last crossover, leave about 3" of bare wire and cut the wire from the spool. Directions for forming the individual petals or leaves will be found with each flower.

The iris is the learning flower for the four-row crossover. You will also find it in the forget-me-not, spring beauty, daisy and African violet.

## Wraparound Loops

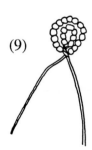

(9)

The wraparound loop is started the same way as the single loop. A second row of beads, however, is wrapped around the first. Measure the required amount of beads for the loop being sure to leave 3" of wire from the knotted end. Make a loop and twist the wires once at the base. Wrap a second row of beads very closely around the outside of the loop. Twist the base 2 times (fig. 9).

If making more than 1 wraparound on 1 wire, make the second loop next to the first, leaving a little room for the extra loop of beads. Wrap the feed wire around the base 1 time, add the second row of beads snugly around this second loop, then wrap the feed wire again 1 time around the base. When finished with the required wraparounds, cut from the spool leaving 3" of wire.

The forget-me-not's petals and the baby's tears are made using the wraparound technique.

## Basic Technique

This technique is used to make larger leaves and petals and can be either rounded or pointed. It is probably the most difficult technique to master — it was for me — but without it, the size and types of flowers are very limited. Under the Procedures section something similar to the following will be seen:

7 bead basic - - 9 rows - - PTRB

Or you might see:

1" basic - -15 rows - - RTRB

First, this tells you how many beads are on the basic wire. Next, it tells you how many rows are needed. Finally, it tells you whether the leaf or petal has a rounded top and rounded bottom (RTRB), or a pointed top and a rounded bottom (PTRB).

Getting Started: Knot the end of your beaded wire and slide the required amount of beads (the basic count) to within 4" of the end. Hold the wire with your left thumb and forefinger under the beads (fig. 10). If you are left-handed, hold the wire with your right hand.

(10)

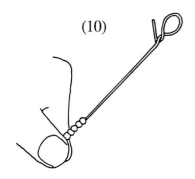

With the bare feed wire in your right hand, make a loop with about 6" of wire. Put your right forefinger in the V under the beads and hold the two wires firmly with your thumb and third finger. Put the four fingers of your left hand in the loop and tightly twist towards you 4 or 5 times. (fig. 11).

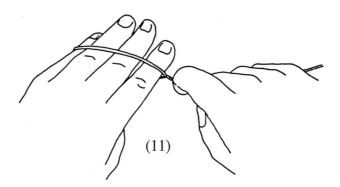

(11)

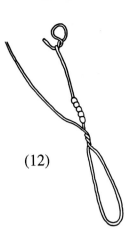

(12)

The number of twists depends on the number of rows called for in the pattern. You now have a top basic and a bottom basic loop (fig. 12). The top basic is the center of the petal or leaf and the bottom basic is the stem. Alays keep the basic wires straight.

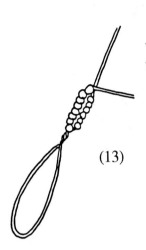

(13)

Round Petals: While holding the basic petal upright in your left hand, bring the feed wire to the left of the basic beads and slide enough beads down to fit from the bottom of the basic beads to the top (fig. 13).

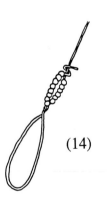

(14)

This first row of beads should fit snugly against the basic beads. Form a 90° angle with the feed wire coming across the front of the basic wire, wrap around the back and across the front again . (fig. 14)

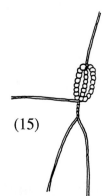

(15)

Forming a right angle across the basic wire makes a rounded petal. Push another row of beads along the right side of the petal to the bottom of the basic. Turn the petal upside down. Being sure to keep the front facing towards you, and forming a 90° angle with the feed wire, wrap around the bottom as you did for the top (fig. 15).

There are now 3 rows. Almost all petals and leaves will have an odd number of rows and will finish at the bottom.

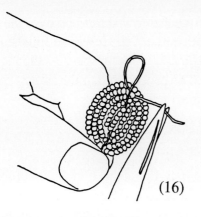

When all the required rows are finished, give the feed wire an extra wrap around the base and cut it as close to the base as possible. Remember to knot the feed wire so the beads on the spool won't fall off. Cut the loop at the bottom so there are 2 stem wires. Cut the knot off the top basic wire, turn the petal over to the back, and push the end of the wire in back of the basic wire between the last two wraps (fig. 16).

(16)

With the needle nose pliers, pull the wire through and back over to the opposite direction. It is important to hold the top of the petal firmly with your thumb and forefinger while pulling the wire through to hold the shape of the petal. Cut the feed wire from the petal as close to the basic wire as possible (fig. 17).

(17)

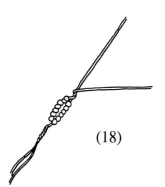

Pointed Petals: The pointed petal and leaf are made the same way as the rounded petal except for a few variations. At the top of the second row, the feed wire should be at a 45° angle to the basic wire and will be 1 or 2 beads longer. Wrap around the basic wire and come back across the front at a 45° angle (fig. 18).

(18)

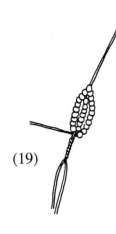

Push the 3rd row of beads up to the top. The top bead of the 3rd row should be over the top bead of the 2nd row (fig. 19). Continue in the same manner until all the rows are finished.

Occasionally, a petal or leaf will have a pointed bottom. The procedure is the same as for the pointed top except, the point begins at the bottom of the third row.

(19)

The poppy is a good flower for practicing the basic technique. It has the rounded petals, which are a bit easier to master, and it has pointed leaves. Continue to make petals and leaves until you are happy with your work before going on to other flowers. I put all of my beginning poppies into the first basket I ever made, and together they look pretty.

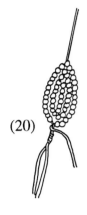

### Reverse Wrap:

So the wires do not show on certain flowers, like the rose petals, you should reverse the direction of the wrap around the basic wire. To do this, simply wrap the feed wire around the back of the basic wire instead of going around the front (fig. 20).

(20)

This is done either at the top or bottom of the petal or leaf.

### Basic Hints:

Remember to keep your wires straight.

To have a nice compact petal with a minimum of wire showing, keep each row as close as possible to the row before it.

For a firmer control of your beadwork, try wrapping the feed wire around your right hand several times — beads and all. This will also keep your hands from slipping.

To make a tight wrap around the top basic, try using your thumbnail to guide the wire as you wrap it around the basic wire.

To keep the bottom round and tight, hold the feed wire tightly at a 90° angle to the basic wire. Using the side of your right forefinger as a guide, turn the petal around with your left hand.

## ADDITIONAL TECHNIQUES

### Single Beaded Wire

This technique is used for flower centers or other parts that have spikes. To make a single beaded wire, twist the end of the beaded wire 5 times around a needle and push the coils together. Remove the needle and cut the "tail" close to the coil. Slide down the required number of beads and cut from the spool leaving a 3" stem (fig. 21).

(21)

14

**Lacing**

The lily of the valley is the only flower that requires lacing in this book. Its purpose is to help keep the shape of larger petals or leaves and to join 2 or more petals or leaves. I like to use #007 ligature wire, which I buy from an orthodontist, for lacing. It is a very fine wire which is strong and does not break when bent. I've also used #32 goldine wire, which works well but does break more easily.

Cut a piece of wire from the spool at least 3 times as long as the area to be laced, plus a few extra inches. Hold the petal facing you with the top pointed up. Starting on the right side of the petal, insert about 2" of wire between the first and second row and between two beads. Bend the two wires to the right (fig. 22), and wrap the longer wire twice around the first row. This will secure the wires.

(22)

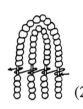

The longer wire goes underneath the 2nd row and up between the 2nd and 3rd rows. Pull it back and down between the 1st and 2nd rows. It then goes underneath the 3rd row, up between the 3rd and 4th rows, and back and down between the 2nd and 3rd rows (fig. 23).

(23)

Continue until you come to the end of the last row and make an extra wrap around the last wire to secure it. Be careful to make sure that the lacing is as straight as possible. Cut both wires close to the beads. This is basically a back stitch. Make sure the front of the petal faces you and that the lacing wire only shows on the back of the petal.

## ASSEMBLING THE FLOWERS AND ARRANGEMENTS

The directions for each individual flower describes how to put it together. Below, however, are a few guidelines and techniques which may be helpful.

**Floral Tape:** I used the light green floral tape for the book's photographs. It comes on 1/2" wide rolls and becomes tacky when stretched. For all of the flowers and arrangements in this book, the tape is cut lengthwise in half. This may seem like a lot of trouble, but the end result is a very delicate looking flower stem. Stretch the tape after it is cut from the roll, either before or after you cut it in half. Cover all leaf stems, flower stems and stem wires with floral tape while the flower is being assembled. As the tape is tacky and will dull the beads, it is a good idea to do all your taping at one time, washing your hands before handling the beads.

To cover the stem wire, place the tape diagonally at the top of the wire-or base of the leaf or petal- and twirl the stem. All individual stems of petals and leaves should be taped, even if the stem will also be coverd with tape. This helps to hold them in place. Bare wires tend to slip around too much. A leaf that has not been taped can be easily pulled from the stem. If you run out of tape, simply add another piece where the first one ended.

When taping down a stem that has a number of wires, there are a few thing to keep in mind. First, the stem wires should always hang straight. Be sure to straighten the wires as you go along as this makes a smooth stem. Secondly, when there are several wires on a stem, it will be necessary to taper them. To do this, fan thewires out and cut at different lenghts. Then straighten and tape the wires.

**Arrangements:** There are several different ways to arrange the miniature flowers in this book. When making a bouquet, like the thistle and marigold, start by binding 3 flowers together about 1" or so below the last leaf with #32 goldine wire or #007 ligature wire. One flower head should be slightly higher than the other two. Add 1 or 2 flowers at a time and space them evenly around the central flowers and a little lower. Wrap tightly several times with the wire after each additional flower is in place. When 6-8 flowers have been bound together, tape the stem to cover the wire. This will keep the wires from slipping. When the last flower is wired, cut the binding wire and tape the bouquet with floral tape completely down the stem. It does not matter if the stem is thick because it's going to be "planted."

To make a bundle like the spring beauty, the daisy or the African violet, the process is basically the same. Cut a piece of #16 or #18 stem wire about 6" long and cover with floral tape. Attach the taller flowers to the stem wire with the binding wire then add the shorter flowers around the outside. The flowers are attached to the stem wire directly under the bottom stem bead. Remember to tape the stem after adding several flowers. The leaves are then added around the outside of the flowers. Tape the stem completely and "plant."

Flowers like the poppy can be treated like a bouquet, placed loose in a miniature vase, or they can be arranged in a line. I have seen them in an "L" and an "S" formation and they were very attractive.

**Planting your flowers:** Probably one of the hardest part of finishing your flower is finding the perfect container. Basically, anything will do: little baskets, saki cups, votive candle holders, small lotus bowls, little clay pots, shells or little vases. Whenever you're shopping, keep an eye out for something that might do. If it isn't right for what you're making now, it will be perfect for something in the future.

For the arrangements in this book, floral clay or modeling clay that won't harden are used to hold the flowers in the container. If the clay is cold and difficult to cut and mold, it can be made softer by putting it in the microwave for a few seconds. Cut up the clay into small pieces and pack into your container. Pack it firmly, but be careful not to break the container. When the clay is about 1/4" from the top of the container, make a small mound in the center. Put some craft glue, either the clear or the white will do, over the clay and cover it with the moss. Make a hole in the center of the container with your awl and insert your arrangement. An awl is useful for pushing the wrapped stems down below the surface. If the stem is too long, you will need heavy duty wire cutters to cut it to the proper length. I find that the wire cutting part of the large pliers works well.

**Care of Your Beaded Flowers:** These flowers are almost care-free. An occasional feather dusting will keep them looking bright for a long time. Eventually, they will begin to get dull and grimy and will require a cleaning. There are two main ways to clean these little flowers.

Fill a bowl with warm water and add a small amount of liquid detergent. Wrap the base of the container with plastic wrap, turn the arrangement upside down and swish in the soapy water. Rinse in clear water and allow to drip dry.

A second way – and this is good for larger arrangements – is to lean or hold the container over the sink and spray with glass cleaner, then rinse with clear water and let drip dry.

Since your arrangement is in floral clay, you can take it out of the container and add to it, or you can take it apart and use the flowers in something else.

### THISTLE

The thistle is a good flower for the beginner. It is easy to do, will get your fingers used to working with beads and wire, and makes a cute arrangement. The technique is the loop, and can be done in any color or a combination of two colors. I used pink and white pearl beads for these, my very first beaded flowers.

| Materials: | 11° pink and white beads for the flower. |
| --- | --- |
| | 11° transparent green bead for calyx and leaves. |
| | #26 wire for the calyx and leaves. |
| | #28 wire for the petals. |
| | #32 for binding. |
| | Light green floral tape. |
| | Small container, floral clay and moss. |

| Procedure | Petals: Center - - 3/4" loop - - 5 on 1 wire in white. |
| --- | --- |
| | Outer - 1" loop - - 8 on 1 wire in pink. |
| | Make 1 white and 1 pink for each flower. |
| | Leave 4" of wire for the stem. |
| | Calyx: 3/4" loop - - 4 on 1 wire in green. |
| | Make 2 for each flower. |
| | Leaves: 1" loop - - 4 on 1 wire in green. |
| | Make 3 for each flower. |

### Assembly of Flower

Twist the 2 wires of the center petals together 2 times to form a circle. Close the loops slightly and curl the petals inward. A small awl is useful for curling the petals. Close the loops slightly on the outer petals and curl. Put the center petals in the middle of the outer petals and twist the two sets of wires at the base of the flower

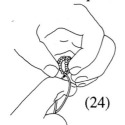

several times. To do this, hold the base of the flower with the tips of your fingers. The flower will be facing the palm of your hand and your fingers will be cupped over. With the forefinger of your other hand inserted in the V of the wires, twist the head of the flower towards you 2 times (fig. 24).

(24)    This will make a nice tight twist. Wrap the calyx around the base of the flower and twist the 2 sets of wires together.

To form the leaves, close each loop and push all 4 loops together to resemble a fan. Twist the wires together and tape down the stem about 2".

Begin taping down the flower stem at the base of the calyx under the flower. Tape on the first leaf with the tip even with the base of the calyx. All the leaves will have a 1/2" stem. Continue wrapping the stem and add the second leaf on the south side of the first leaf. The tip should be even with the base of the first leaf. Add the third leaf in the same manner on the east side of the second leaf and wrap the stem another 3". The leaves should come out from the stem a little and face up.

To make an arrangement you will need from 13 to 17 flowers. Put the flowers together forming a bouquet and plant following the directions for Assembling the Flowers and Arrangements.

# MINI MARIGOLD

The Mini Marigold is another flower which uses the loop technique. It is less formal than the thistle, and makes a very bright arrangement when transparent orange and yellow beads are used.

Materials:
11° orange and yellow beads for the flower.
11° transparent green bead for calyx and leaves.
#26 wire for the calyx and leaves.
#28 wire for the petals.
#32 for binding.
Light green floral tape.
Small container, floral clay and moss

Procedure
Petals: 1st row - - 12 bead loop - - 5 on 1 wire.
2nd row - - 14 bead loop - - 8 on 1 wire.
Make 6 orange and 6 yellow.
Leave 4" of wire for the stem.
Calyx: 10 bead loop - - 5 on 1 wire in green.
Make 1 for each flower.
Leaves: 3" loop in green.
Make 2 for each flower.

## Assembly of Flower

Close the loops of the first row of petals and curl them inward. Do the same for the second row and attach it around the first row. Twist the two sets of wires together in the same way as the thistle. Wrap the calyx around the base of the flower and twist the wires together again. The flower should resemble a ball.

(25)

To form the leaves, close the loop and twist 3 times (fig. 25). Tape about 1/2" of the stem.

Begin taping the stem of the flower at the base of the calyx and add the first leaf about 3/4" down. The leaf should show above the flower. There is no leaf stem. Add the second leaf on the opposite side of the first about 3/4" further down the stem. Bend the leaves out slightly from the stem. Finish taping down the stem for 3".

To make an arrangement, bind the flowers together alternating yellow and orange to form a bouquet. Plant in a container following the directions on Assembling the Flowers and Arrangements.

19

# IRIS

There are so many colors and combinations of colors one can use in making the iris, that just about anything goes. The ones shown here are made with a 3X sapphire blue bead, but they also look good in a transparent, lined or iris bead. This is a good flower for learning the four-row crossover technique.

Materials:    11° bead for the top and bottom petals.
14° opaque yellow for the beard. *
11° transparent green for bud calyx and leaves.
#26 wire for the calyx and leaves.
#28 wire for the petals.
Light green floral tape.
Small container, floral clay and moss.
* (11° may be substituted)

Procedure

Flower: Top petals - - 1-1/4" loop - - four-row crossover.
Make 3 on 1 wire.
Bottom petals:  1-1/2" loop - - four-row crossover - - 3 on 1 wire.
Beard: 1/2" loop - - wrap around once, - - 3 on 1 wire.
Bud: 1" loop - - four-row crossover.
Make 1 for each flower in the same color.
Bud Calyx: 10 bead loop  - - 3 on 1 wire in green.
Leaves: 2-1/2" loop - - four-row crossover - - make 2.
2-3/4" loop - - four-row crossover - - make 1.
* To substitute 11° bead for the beard, make a 1/2" loop – 3 on 1 wire. It will not be necessary to wrap around once.

## Assembly of Flower

The flower is made in 3 sections. Place the top petal on the beard and twist the wires, making sure the petals are close together. Add the bottom petals under the beard and twist as close to the base as possible. Flatten the leaves and tape the stems 1/2". Tape the flower stem and attach the first shorter leaf with the tip even with the base of the flower. The leaves have no stems. Add the second shorter leaf south of the first leaf with the tip midway down the first leaf. Add the third leaf east of the second and midway down. Bend the leaves out slightly.  Flatten the top 3 petals and curl upwards until they almost touch at the tips. Flatten the 3 bottom petals and turn down. The beard turns down slightly. The 3 layers of petals should be aligned (fig. 26).

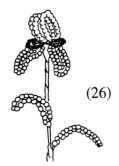

(26)

Attach the calyx to the bud and twist the bud into a spiral. Attach leaves the same as the flower. Tape 3 flowers and 2 buds together below the bottom leaves.

The iris looks good with 3-5 flowers planted in a small container. A friend of mine, however, has at least 25 different colored irises in one pot and it is beautiful!

# FORGET-ME-NOT

The forget-me-not makes an appealing little arrangement. Observant students will notice that it, along with most of these flowers, has done a bit of evolving from the original flower that Mother Nature made. I'm sure she won't mind a few changes for the sake of design and simplicity. The wraparound technique is used with this flower. Basically, any bead color or type can be used. I made this arrangement with a 14° opaque cornflower - blue bead. Using the 11° bead will make a larger flower.

Materials:    11° or 14° bead for the flower.
11° transparent pale green for the stem.
11° yellow pearl or ceylon bead for the center.
11° transparent medium green bead for the leaves.
#26 wire for leaves.
#28 wire for the petals.
#32 wire for binding.
Light green floral tape.
Small container, floral clay and moss.

## Procedure

Flower: 5 bead loop - - wraparound once.
4 on 1 wire.
1 yellow bead for center.
Stem: Bead down stem wires with pale green. Use 4 different lengths ranging from 1" to 1-3/4".
Leaves: 3" loop - - four-row crossover. Make 1 for each shorter stemmed flower.
4" loop - - four-row crossover. Make 1 for each longer stemmed flower.

## Assembly of Flower

Be sure to leave at least 3" of wire before making the flowers. After the petals are made, pull one stem wire up through 2 petals, add 1 yellow bead and bring the stem wire back down the opposite side. This makes a quick and easy center. Twist the 2 wires together 2 to 3 times under the flower. To add the pale green beads to the stem, cut the wire from the spool. Add the measured amount of beads on the 2 stem wires and push them all the way up to the base of the flower. The finished arrangement will have 4 different heights of flowers.

Twist 1 flower and 1 leaf together at the base of the beaded stem. The shorter leaves go with the shorter flowers. Then twist 2 groups together. Make at least 7 groups (14 flowers), or more, to fit your container. Tape each group of flowers and wrap together with #32 wire to make a bouquet, putting the taller flowers in the center. Tape the stem again and plant in your container.

## POPPY

The poppy should be the flower to choose to learn the basic technique. My first poppies were rather pathetic. My teacher made me do poppies until I got the technique under control before she let me go on to something else. For weeks I made poppies until finally I was able to present, with very sore fingers, one adequate poppy. Once again, people aren't going to come running up and say, "Oh, what cute poppies," but the resemblance is close enough. I chose transparent red for these poppies with opaque black for the centers, but they also look good in yellow, orange, white or blue.

Materials:   11° bead for the flower.
14° opaque black or yellow for the center. It is ok to substitute 11° with no noticeable difference.
11° transparent green bead for the leaves.
#26 wire for the petals, calyx and leaves .
#18 stem wire.
Light green floral tape.
Small container, floral clay and moss.

Procedure

Petals: 5 bead basic - - 9 rows - - RTRB  make 5
Remember, RTRB means rounded top; rounded bottom.
Center: 3/4" loop, 5 on 1 wire use #28 wire.
Calyx: 3/4" loop, 5 on 1 wire.
Leaves: 7 bead basic - - 7 rows - - PTRB make 2.
7 bead basic - - 9 rows - - PTRB - - make 2.
Bud:  Make 1 petal and 1 9-row leaf.

### Assembly of Flower

Stack the 5 petals right side up, making sure they are even. While holding the stem wires with pliers, grasp the petals and twist towards you 3 times. Use pliers to tighten the twist if necessary. With the front side of the petals facing you, bring the first petal down and twist to the left. Bring the second one down and twist to the right. The third petal comes down and to the left; the fourth down and to the right;  the fifth goes straight up. Make sure the petals are evenly spaced and are facing in. Cup the petals slightly.

Put the center in the middle of the petals and pull the wires through so they are underneath the flower. Twist just those two wires and make sure all the wires are hanging straight. Attach the calyx under the flower petals and twist the ires several times around the stem wires.Tape the stem about 1". Cut a piece of stem wire 6" long and tape. Insert one end into the flower stem wires and tape down just enough to make it secure. Taper the stem wires by fanning them out and cutting at different lengths. Be sure to straighten the wires again.

Tape down the leaf stems about 1". Attach the first smaller leaf so the tip is even with the middle of the petals. All the leaves will have a 1/2" stem. The second leaf is opposite the first and the tip is even with the middle of the first leaf. The third bigger leaf is opposite the second, and the fourth is opposite the third. Finish taping down the stem.

The bud is made by stacking the petal on top of the leaf and twisting the stem wires – similar to twisting the petals. Grasp the leaf and petal at the base and spiral. The leaf should be on the outside,  with some of the flower color showing through. There is no calyx and the leaves are attached the same as the flower's leaves.

These poppies can be arranged loosely in a miniature vase. They can also be arranged into a line. To do this, omit the 6" #18 stem wire and attach them with binding wire to a long #16 stem wire. Buds should be attached first with some leaves, then add the flowers and more leaves. Five flowers on one wire and three flowers on another wire can be bent into an attractive "S" or "L" - shaped arrangement.

# ADDITIONAL DESIGNS

## AFRICAN VIOLET

This is probably one of my favorite flowers to make. The finished plant looks like it's alive, the way it quivers when picked up or touched. The flowers come in such a wide range of colors from white, pink, yellow, blue and purple, that it's easy to find a color to make.

Materials:       11° transparent, lined or cut bead for the flower – anything "formal".
11° yellow Ceylon or pearl bead for the center.
11° transparent light green for the stem.
11° transparent green.
4mm transparent green pony bead.
#28 wire for the petals.
#26 wire for the leaves.
Floral tape, container, floral clay and moss.

Procedure

Flower: 1" loop - - four-row crossover - - 5 on 1 wire.  Add 2 yellow beads for the center.
Bead down stem with light green 2-1/4", 2", 1-3/4" and 1-1/2".
Make 12.
Bud: 3/4" loop - - four row crossover.
Add 1 pony bead under calyx.
Bead down stem same as flower.
Make 1 bud for every 3 flowers.
Calyx: 10 bead loop - - 3 on 1 wire.
Make 1 for each bud.
Leaves: 6 bead basic - - 9 rows - - PTRB - - make 3.
6 bead basic - - 11 rows - - PTRB - - make 3.
6 bead basic - - 13 rows - - PTRB - - make 4.
6 bead basic - - 15 rows - - PTRB - - make 4.
6 bead basic - 17 rows - - PTRB - - make 5.
Add 1" beads to the bottom basic loop.

* Please read about the leaves before beginning.

## Assembly of Flower

Leave long stem wires when making the flowers. After the flower is completed, pull 1 stem wire up between two petals. Then add 2 yellow beads, place in the center of the flower and pull the wire back down through the opposite petals. Twist the 2 wires snugly under the flower. Add the pale green stem beads at various lengths. The flowers have no calyx.

To make the bud, add a calyx under the four-row crossover as close to the beads as possible and twist the 4 wires together. Spiral the bud. Cut 1 calyx wire and 1 flower stem wire close to the twist. Add 1 pony bead under the calyx to cover the twists and bead down the stem with the pale green bead the same lengths as the flower. Make 1 bud for every 3 flowers. Twist 2 flowers together and twist 1 flower and 1 bud together. Then twist the 2 sets together for a group of 3 flowers and 1 bud, and tape the stem.

Leaves: Before forming the bottom basic loop, measure 1" beads and include them in the loop. They will slide around (fig. 27).

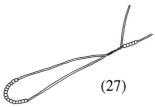

(27)

When the leaf is finished, do not cut the feed wire. Cut one side of the loop close to the twist, being careful that the beads do not fall off. Measure 1" of beads from the feed wire and slide the beads up and parallel to the beads on the bottom basic wire (fig. 28). Twist the wires at the base of the stem beads and cut the feed wire from the spool, leaving at least 2" of bare wire.

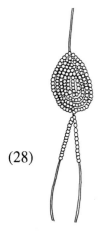

(28)

Twist the 2 beaded wires 3 times (fig. 29).

Tape a piece of #18 stem wire that is long enough to fit the container. Start binding the flowers to the stem wire making sure that the bottom of the beaded stems are even with the top of the stem wire. Put the taller flowers in the middle and the shorter flowers around the outside. Add the leaves one at a time. Bind on the smallest ones evenly around the base of the flowers, then add the next size in between. Continue until you end with the largest leaves on the bottom. The leaves are pointed down. Tape the stem and plant in your container.

I think it is easier to shape the flower petals after they are in a container. Using your small awl, flatten each petal and curl. Alternate curling 1 petal up and 1 petal down. There will be 2 petals together that curl either up or down.

A smaller version can be made by making 5 flowers and 2 buds and adding 10 to 12 smaller leaves.

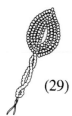

(29)

# BABY'S BREATH

Baby's breath adds lightness and airiness to many beaded flower bouquets and arrangements. In this book, several small sprays are added to a bouquet of miniature tea roses.

Materials:      14° opaque white bead
                           #30 gold wire

Procedure: Approximately 8" from the end of the knotted wire make a 5 bead loop. Twist the two wires for 1/2". In order to have tight loops and even twists, turn the loop instead of the wire. On the left side of the twisted wires – which is the stem – make another 5 bead loop 1/2" out and twist back to the stem. On the right side of the stem make a 3rd 5 bead loop 1/2" out and twist back to the stem (A). Twist down the stem for 3/4". Make another 5 bead loop 1" out to the left of the stem and continue as above for the 3 loops (B). Do another group of 3 loops 1" out on the right of the stem (C). Twist down the stem 3/4" and follow the same procedure for (D) (E) and (F). Twist down the stem for 2" (fig. 30).

*11° opaque or ceylon white can be used. Make a 3 bead loop instead of the 5 bead loop. Everything else will be the same.

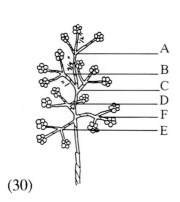

(30)

This makes 1 small spray which can be taped to a piece of stem wire and added to a miniature bouquet. To make a large spray, make 3 or more units of A-C and tape to stem wire as illustrated in figure 31.

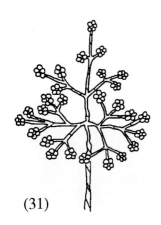

(31)

25

## BABY'S TEARS

I wanted to include baby's tears in this collection because it makes such a unique arrangement by itself and can add interest to a bouquet of different flowers. I used 14° transparent green bead, but if 11° is all you have, please use it. The only result will be a bigger plant. If you use the 11°bead, go with a #28 wire to hold up the fronds.

Materials:        14° opaque white bead.
14° transparent green bead
#32 gold wire.

Procedure: Leave 8" of bare stem wire. Make 1 7-bead loop and wrap around once. Cut off the knot at the end of the wire. Bead down both wires with 7 beads. When making the round leaves, use just the feed wire. To the left of the stem, make a 7-bead loop and wrap around once. Make another leaf on the right side of the stem. Add 5 white beads to the bare wire and make a loop in the center of the stem between the two leaves (fig. 32). Be sure the loop is lying flat against the stem. Bead down both wires with 7 beads.

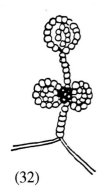

* If you are using 11° beads and want to have a smaller plant, make a 5 bead loop, wrap around once. Only use 5 beads for the stem and make a 3 bead loop for the center white "flower".

Baby's tears can be made in many different lengths. Twist 2 together and tape to a small piece of #18 stem wire to make the stem strong enough to stick into the clay. Plant at different locations in your container, having some of the fronds trailing over the edge at varying lengths, and some upright. They should be somewhat floppy.

(32)

# MINI CALLA LILY

This makes a cute little arrangement that is quick and easy to do.

Materials:

14° opaque white for the flower.
14° opaque yellow for the center.
11° transparent crystal for the leaves.
11° transparent green for the leaves.
#28 gold wire for the flower.
#28 green enamel wire for the leaves.
Floral tape, container, floral clay and moss.

Procedure

Flower: 5 bead basic - - 11 rows - - RTPB - - make 3.
Make the bottom very pointed.
Center: 1" loop in yellow - - spiral - - make 3.
Leaves: 1-1/32" basic - - 3 rows PTRB - - make 2.
1-3/4" basic - - 3 rows - - PTRB - - make 2.
2" basic - - 3 rows - PTRB - - make 2.
2-1/4" basic - - 3 rows - - PTRB - - make 1.

Put the transparent green bead on the green wire, then add the crystal bead for the basic amount.

* If you are using 11° beads and the basic bead count, the flower will be bigger. The yellow center loop should change from 1" to 1-1/2", making it bigger also. If you want a smaller flower, change the count to 3 basic – 9 rows. The yellow center will remain at 1".

## Assembly of Flower

After the white flower petal is made, put the yellow center in the middle with the top third down from the tip of the flower. push the center stem wire through the front of the flower and out the back next to the central stem and twist the 4 wires several times. Fold the base of the flower making the 2 sides meeet and tape the stems. Make the flower stems 1", 1/2" and 1/4" long. The leaves will have 2 rows of crystal beads in the center. Attach the leaves of random lenghts at the same point around the base and curl them down slightly. Plant in your container.

# CROCUS

Not only is the crocus one of the earliest flowers to bloom, it is one of my first designs. I was so glad to see them that I picked one of each color, got out my beads and went to work. Designing a flower really draws you into it and you begin to notice things that only a bee would see.

Materials:    11° transparent or pearl bead - - white, purple and yellow for the petals.
11° transparent orange for the pistol.
14° opaque yellow for the stamen.  The stamen may be made with an 11° bead. There will be no change in the appearance of the flwer.
11° transparent crystal and green for the leaves.
#28 gold wire for the center.
#26 gold wire for the petals.
#28 green enamel wire for the leaves.
#32 binding wire
Floral tape, container, floral clay and moss.

## Procedure

Petals: 3/4" basic -- 9 rows -- RTPB -- make 3.
3/4" basic --11 rows -- RTPB -- make 3.
Center: Pistol -- 3 7-bead loops on 1 wire -- bead down stem 3/4" with 11° transparent orange -- make 1.
Stamen - single beaded wire with 1/2" 14/0 opaque yellow -- make 3
Leaves: 3-1/2" basic -- 3 rows -- PTRB -- make 4.
Add 3-1/2" crystal transparent bead to the green enamel wire that is already beaded with the green – this is the basic count – then make the 2 rows in green.

## Assembly of Flower

Please note that the petals have rounded tops and pointed bottoms. Start cupping the petals slightly after the 5th row. To do this, reduce by 1 bead when wrapping around the top and bottom basics. Stack the 3 smaller petals and twist the wires at the base several times. The front of the petals should be facing out. Twist 2 stamen together, then twist 1 stamen and the pistol together. Twist these 2 groups and put in the center of the small petals between 2 leaves. Twist the wires around the petal wires. Stack the 3 larger petals and twist the wires at the base making sure the front of the petals face out. Put the smaller petals and center in the larger petals between 2 leaves. Using your pliers, twist all the wires together. This makes the stem as narrow as possible. Adjust the petals so the outer ones are between the inner ones and not aligned. Taper the stem wires and tape down 2". Bind on the 4 leaves 1" down from the base of the flower and tape. The leaves go up and curve out slightly. Plant the flower so the base of the leaves appear to be coming out of the ground.

# LILY OF THE VALLEY

These flowers are very dear to me and I always look forward to seeing them come up in the spring. As the leaves are large, they will need to be laced. Just be sure to keep the visible stitches on the back of the leaf.

Materials:    14° opaque white bead for the buds and flowers.
11° transparent yellow for the center.
11° transparent green for the calyx and leaves.
#28 gold wire for the flowers.
#28 green enamel wire for the leaves.
#32 wire for lacing and binding.
Floral tape, container, floral clay and moss.

*11° white beads can be substituted. If using the size 11° bead the loops will not close as tightly. Reduce the number of loops on the flower from 6 to 5 on 1 wire.

Procedure    Bud #1: 1/4" loop -- 3 on 1 wire -- curl into a ball.
Make 1 for each flower.
Bud #2: 3/8" loop -- 4 on 1 wire.
Add 1 yellow bead to the center.
Close loops and curl petals in.
Make 1 for each flower.
Flower: 1/2" loop -- 6 on 1 wire.
Close loops and curl petals in forming a cup.
Make 4 for each flower.
Center: 1 single beaded wire with 3 transparent yellow beads.
Leaves: 2" basic -- 13 rows -- PTRB-- make 2.
2-1/2" basic -- 15 rows -- PTRB -- make 1.
Leave 3 long wires.
Lace 2 times.

## Assembly of Flower

Leave 8" long stem wires for the buds. Tape the stem of the first bud and turn the head downward. Before curling the petals of the second bud, pull 1 stem wire through 2 petals, add 1 yellow bead to the center, then pull the wire back down through the opposite petals. Twist wires close to the base. Close the petal loops and curl them in slightly forming a cup. Tape down the stem 1". To form the flower, put the single beaded wire (center) into the middle and pull the wire through the bottom. Twist the 3 wires 2 times close to the base. Cut 1 wire to make the stem thinner and tape 1" making sure the tape covers all the wires. Close the petal loops and curl in slightly.

Attach the second bud 1/2" below the first bud with floral tape. Leave about 1/4" stem and turn the bead down. Tape the first flower 1/2" below bud #2 leaving about 1/4" stem and turn the head down. Continue for the other 3 flowers and tape the stem 3".

Make the rows of the leaves as close together as possible and start cupping them after the 7th row. To do this, remove one bead when you reach the top basic and bottom basic wires and pull, so the next bead is in its place before wrapping around the basic wire. Each leaf is laced two times, dividing it evenly into thirds. Be sure the laciing is straight across the leaf and that the stitches show on the back only. Tape the 3 stem wires on each leaf.

To make a bouquet, you should have 5 flower stalks and 3 leaves. Bind the flowers together about 1-1/2" below the last flower and tape. In baack of the flowers add the two smaller leaves. Wire them to the flowers so the abse of the the base of the leaves are even with the binding wire on the flowers. Add the larger leaf behind the smaller ones and centered between them. Tape the stem and plant.

# DAISY

This is another flower that has done some evolving. I tried to make a miniature replica of the real thing, but it just didn't look right. Of course, the petals can be done in any color. I make what I call a black-eyed Susan using the same procedure, but with opaque yellow for the petals and opaque brown for the center.

Materials:  14° opaque white for petals.
14° opaque yellow for the center.
4mm transparent green pony bead - 1 for each flower and leaf.
11° transparent pale green and medium green.
#26 wire for center and leaves.
#28 for petals.
#18 stem wire.
Floral tape, floral clay, moss and container.

Procedure

Petals: 1" loop -- four-row crossover -- 8 on 1 wire.
Leave 4" stem wires Make 5.
Center: 2 bead basic -- 5 rows -- RTRB.
Do not cut top basic wire. Wire is needed on each end for attaching.
Leave 1 long wire on bottom by cutting one side of the bottom basic loop at the twist.
Leaves: 3-1/2" loop -- four-row crossover. Make 5.
Add 1 pony bead at base of leaf and 4 pale green beads.
* If you are using 11° opaque white beads for the petals, make only 6 1" loop – four crossovers on 1 wire. For the yellow center, make the same count as the 14°. The center will be only slighty bigger

## Assembly of Flower

Close the finished petals into a circle by bringing 1 wire under the last petal, up and over the next petal, and back down. Attach the center to the petals by placing it in the middle and pulling the wires through, making sure the wires are hidden between the petals. Twist the 4 wires together underneath the flower as close to the base as possible. Cut 1 petal wire and 1 center wire. Add 1 pony bead and push it up the stem and over the twist. Bead down the stem at varying lengths from 2" to 1-1/4" with the pale green bead. Twist 2 flowers together and twist 3 together. Tape the stems. Also tape the leaf stems and a piece of #18 stem wire. Bind the two groups of flowers together onto the stem wire under the last bead of the stem, then add the leaves around the base. Plant in your container.

## SPRING BEAUTY

I enjoy making this flower not only because it's such a cheerful little thing, but also because it's relatively quick to do. You can make the arrangement as big or small as you want, but be sure to increase it in increments of three. I used a two-toned lined pink bead, but any pink or white transparent bead will do.

Materials:   11° bead for the petals.
11° yellow bead - - 1 per flower.
4mm transparent green pony bead - - 1 per flower and bud.
11° light green for stems and medium green for the leaves.
#28 wire for the petals.
#28 green enamel wire for the leaves.
Floral tape, container, floral clay and moss.

Procedure

Flower: 13 bead loop, wraparound once - 5 on 1 wire.
Close the loop before the second wrap and leave long stem wires.
1 yellow bead for the center.
Make 6 for a small arrangement.
Calyx: 9 bead loop - - 5 on 1 #26 wire.
Make 1 for each flower and bud.
Bud: 13 bead loop - - four-row crossover.
Make 1 bud for every 3 flowers.
Leaves: 2-1/2" basic - - 3 rows - - PTRB - -1 for each flower.
The green enamel wire is much stiffer than the brass and will help hold the leaf shape.

Assembly of Flower

Be sure to leave long stem wires – at least 3-1/2". After the petals are made, pull one stem wire up through 2 petals, add 1 yellow bead, and bring the stem wire back down through the opposite petals. Put calyx under each flower and bud and twist 2 times towards you. Cut one calyx wire and one flower wire close to the base. Add one pony bead under the calyx. Bead down the stems at different lengths – 2-1/4", 2", 1-3/4" and 1-1/2" with the pale green beads. Twist 2 flowers together and then twist 1 flower and 1 bud together. Twist them all together to form a group of 3 flowers and 1 bud. Tape the stem. You will need at least 2 groups to make a small arrangement. Bend the flower heads down a little. Add the leaves at the base of the flower stems and bend them downward and curve slightly . Bend several leaves up among the flowers. Be sure that each leaf is closed and does not gape. Plant in your container.

## MINIATURE TEA ROSE

These little roses are made with a darker center for contrast. I've also added baby's breath to the arrangement to give it an airy appearance.

Materials:　11° transparent dark rose for the center.
11° transparent light rose for the outer petals.
11° transparent green for the calyx and leaves.
#26 gold wire for the petals, calyx and leaves.
Floral tape, container, floral clay and moss

Procedure

Petals: Center --4 bead basic -- 7 rows -- RTRB --- make 2.
Outer -- 5 bead basic -- 9 rows -- RTRB -- make 4.
Reverse wrap on the bottom basic.
Make the petals tight and cup.
Calyx: 20 bead loop -- four-row crossover - 5 on 1 wire.
Make 1 for each flower.
Leaves: 6 bead basic -- 9 rows -- PTRB -- make 1.
6 bead basic -- 7 rows -- PTRB -- make 2.

**Assembly of Flower**

Fold the 2 center petals in the middle with the front side facing out. Fit the 2 together, twist the wires and tape. To form the outer petals, cup the base with the front side facing out and curl the top of the petal back. This hides the top basic wires. Attach two petals to the center opposite each other and wrap with binding wire. Add the other two petals opposite each other covering the edges of the first two. Tape about 1". Attach the calyx directly under the flower head. Twist the calyx wires and leave them hanging straight. Bend the points of the calyx back and down. Tape down the stem.

To make the leaf branch, tape the larger leaf stem and add the 2 smaller leaves directly opposite each other, about 1/2" down the stem. Bend the leaves to a 90° angle to the stem and tape. The leaf will have a 1" stem. Attach to the flower stem allowing the tip of the leaf to show above the top of the flower and tape the stem.

I think these look good formed into a bouquet with sprays of Baby's Breath and put into a small vase.

**Other books by Promenade Publishing:**

**Beaded Clothing Techniques** by Therese Spears　　　ISBN 0-932255-01-9

**Contemporary Loomed Beadwork** by Therese Spears　　　ISBN 0-932255-02-7

**Flash Jewely Making Techniques** by Therese Spears　　　ISBN 0-932255-03-5

**Beaded Dream Catchers** by Mary R. Musgrove　　　ISBN 0-932255-05-1

**Beaded Earrings** by Therese Spears　　　ISBN 0-932255-00-0